Goldfish

MC

Goldfish

Written by
Carl Cozier

Mason Crest
450 Parkway Drive, Suite D
Broomall, PA 19008
www.masoncrest.com
Developed and produced by Mason Crest

Printed and bound in the United States of America.

First printing
9 8 7 6 5 4 3 2 1

Series ISBN: 978-1-4222-3691-8
ISBN: 978-1-4222-3697-0
ebook ISBN: 978-1-4222-8089-8

Words in bold are explained in the glossary on page 127.

QR CODES AND LINKS TO THIRD PARTY CONTENT

Understanding and Caring for Your Pet

Aquarium

Cats

Dog Training

Ferrets

Gerbils

Goldfish

Guinea Pigs

Hamsters

Kittens

Parakeets

Puppies

Rabbits

 Educational Videos: Readers can view videos by scanning our QR codes, providing them with additional educational content to supplement the text. Examples include news coverage, moments in history, speeches, iconic moments, and much more!

 Words to Understand: These words with their easy-to-understand definitions will increase the reader's understanding of the text, while building vocabulary skills.

Contents

The First Goldfish

The Chinese first caught fish from the wild 4,500 years ago, and kept them as a source of food.

The history of the goldfish.

The crucian carp (Carassius carassius), a small brown-colored fish, was a frequent sight in the cool, slow-moving freshwater rivers and streams of southern China. The Chinese caught carp from the wild, and then set up their own fish farms to breed and sell as food. Fish farmers noticed that some fish were brighter in color, more orange than brown, and they decided to breed these fish to produce gold-colored fish.

By the time of the Chinese Sung Dynasty, 1,000 years ago, the goldfish was recognised as a species in its own right. But goldfish were not for eating. They were kept in beautiful ponds, planted with water lilies. Soon keeping fish was a popular hobby among the Chinese.

The Japanese koi (pictured below) may look like the goldfish (left), but has in fact descended from a different species of carp and has distinctive whiskers around its mouth.

Fancy Goldfish

The Japanese also caught carp from the wild, and they developed into their own species, known as koi. These are much bigger than goldfish, and come in a dazzling array of colors. Today koi are highly prized all over the world.

In the 14th century, the Japanese turned their fish-breeding skills to goldfish and they developed spectacular new varieties.

They kept their fancy goldfish in ponds, which were decorated with plants and sculptures. Wooden bridges and stepping-stone pathways helped give admirers a really good view of the fish.

Spreading Worldwide

News of fancy goldfish spread outside China and Japan in the 19th century. Ships loaded with goods from the East sailed to Europe. They carried silks and spices, and interesting plants and animals, including fancy goldfish.

In 1853, the world's first public aquarium opened in London. People were fascinated by the fish from the East and fish-keeping became a new hobby.

The first goldfish were exported to North America and Australia in the late 19th century and soon goldfish were the most popular pet fish in the world. In fact, they rank among the most popular of all pets, with only dogs and cats ahead of them.

Perfect Pets

Hundreds of different fish species are kept in aquariums, but the goldfish is an all-time favorite. What is the secret of its success?

There are many reasons why goldfish are perfect pets.

- Goldfish are beautiful to look at.

- They are inexpensive to buy.

- There are lots of different varieties to choose from.

- They can be kept indoors in an aquarium or outdoors in a pond.

- They do not take up very much room.

- They are one of the most **hardy** of all aquarium fish, and can live for up to 25 years (14 years for the fancy varieties).

- If you suffer from pet allergies, which are caused by having animals with fur in the house, keeping goldfish is the perfect solution.

Good Luck

Keeping fish can have a calming effect on people. In the Chinese system of feng shui, which helps people to live in harmony with their surroundings, goldfish (known as baby dragons) are highly valued. The Chinese word for goldfish is *yu* which is the same as the word for success, so keeping goldfish is believed to bring good luck.

Special Requirements

While it is true that goldfish are relatively easy to keep, and inexpensive to buy and feed, they have specific needs that must be met so they can thrive and live long, healthy lives.

In reality, as a fish owner you are mainly a water keeper. The fish tank is your goldfish's entire world, and you control its environment. You must do partial water changes at least once every two weeks to keep the water from becoming dirty and even **toxic** and un-hygienic for your finned friends. You must ask yourself if you have the time to keep the tank clean and your goldfish healthy. Once you have decided fishkeeping is the right hobby for you, your fish will provide you with years of enjoyment throughout their lives in a well-maintained system.

Even though keeping goldfish is comparatively straightforward, do not be tempted to rush into buying them. Like all living creatures, goldfish have their own special needs.

They must be:

- Housed in a tank that is the correct size for the number of fish you are keeping.

- Kept in fresh, clean water.

- Fed every day.

- Checked regularly to make sure they are in good health.

- In a tank that is routinely cleaned.

- Taken care of when you are on vacation.

Goldfish Homes

Goldfish are coldwater fish, which means they can live in cold water without special heating equipment. However, they are just as comfortable in more temperate water conditions.

In fact, goldfish can live in an outdoor pond all year round, but you will need to select the hardy varieties that can survive in cold temperatures. And pay attention to your local climate, because in some places it gets too cold for goldfish to winter. Ask before you buy a fish for outdoor pond whether it can survive a cold winter in your area.

Goldfish Basics

To look after goldfish, you need to understand how their bodies work.

Brain

Goldfish used to be thought of as the dimwits of the animal kingdom because, among other things, they have a very short memory. However, it has now been shown that a goldfish can recognize members of its own **school**, and knows when it is feeding time.

Nostrils

Goldfish use their sense of smell to find food. They can also smell chemicals in the water.

Eyes

The eyes bulge out slightly, giving the goldfish good all-around vision, even though it cannot turn its head. Compared to many species of fish, the goldfish has ex-cellent vision and can see a distance of 15 feet (4.5 m).

Gills

Goldfish do not have lungs. They use their **gills** to take in oxygen from the water and get rid of carbon dioxide.

Hearing

Goldfish do not have ears as we would recognise them. They have a modified hearing organ located inside the body, called the Weberian apparatus, to amplify sound. Goldfish dislike loud noises, and will dart away to find a safe hiding place.

Color

The distinctive color of the goldfish is made by three types of light-responsive cells. These cells are called melanocytes (black), erythrophores (red), and xanthophores (yellow).

The traditional a sheen of the goldfish is due to a highly reflective material called guanine that is found on and under the scales.

Dorsal fin

This keeps the goldfish stable in the water. It is missing in some fancy varieties, which makes them poor swimmers.

Lateral line

This is a line of cells that runs along the sides of the goldfish and alerts it to any disturbance in the water. The **lateral** line is a sensory organ. The lateral line is extremely sensitive and can detect motion, current, pressure, and even sound.

Caudal fin

The caudal or tail fin is used to propel the goldfish through the water. In fancy varieties the tail is split down the middle to form twin tails.

Scales

The body is covered in bony scales that overlap one another from the head to the tail. This keeps the fish streamlined, so the goldfish can swim more easily.

Pectoral fins

These are located on either side of the goldfish, just behind the gills. They are used for forward and backward propulsion and for stability.

Pelvic fins

These are also on either side of the body, between the pectoral and anal fins. They are used for stability and steering.

Anal fin

There is usually one anal fin on the underside of the body. However, some varieties have a double anal fin.

Vent

This is where the goldfish gets rid of waste.

Goldfish are cold-blooded, which means that their body temperature changes depending on the temperature of the water. They can withstand a wide range of temperatures, as long as there are no sudden changes.

Goldfish Varieties

There are more than 100 varieties of goldfish, so you are certain to find something that you love!

Goldfish come in different sizes, shapes, and colors, but some are much easier to look after than others. If you go for the more exotic varieties, remember that they need special care:

- Single-tail goldfish are tough and hardy. But they can grow quite big and may reach up to 12 inches long (30 cm).

- Fancy goldfish, which include all the twin-tailed varieties, must be kept in an indoor aquarium. They will not survive in a pond (unless you live someplace where it is warm all year around). The temperature should be between 64-73°F (18-23°C). Hardy goldfish can live in temperatures between 50- 75°F (10- 24°C).

- Some fancy varieties have very fine fins, so you will have to be careful with rocks and other objects in the tank, as fins can easily be ripped.

- Twin-tailed goldfish and varieties without a dorsal fin do not swim as well as the single-tailed varieties. They will lose out if they have to compete with other fish for food. It is better not to mix twin-tailed and singled-tailed varieties.

There are too many varieties to show them all in a book this size, but here are some of the types you are most likely to find in your aquarium store.

Check out these goldfish varieties.

Common Goldfish

This is the traditional goldfish, which can be any color ranging from golden red to pale yellow. It is an ideal choice if you are new to fishkeeping. It can live in an aquarium or a pond. Usually these fish are brilliant orange-red or yellow, though young fish are often darker in color.

Shubunkin

This is a beautiful fish with a blue-silver body mottled with black, red, brown, yellow, and violet. They have streamlined bodies with well-developed and even fins. Generally, they do not grow as big as common goldfish. They can also live in an aquarium or a pond.

Shubunkins possess nacreous scales (a mix of metallic and transparent scales that are pearly in appearance). The overlapping patches of red, white, blue, grey, and black (along with dark speckles), which is known as calico, normally extend to the fins of shubunkins.

Comet

Slender in body shape, the comet has a long, single tail fin, which can grow up to 12 inches (30 cm) long.

The comet is more active than most other goldfish breeds and can swim very fast over short distances. It can live in an aquarium or a pond. The comet can be distinguished from the common goldfish by its long, single, and deeply forked tail fin. Comets with yellow, orange, red, white, and red-and-white coloration are common. They were originally bred in the United States.

Ryukin

A goldfish with a short body, a steeply curved back, and flowing fins. It is very round in shape and looks like a butterfly from the rear. This is the easiest of the fancy goldfish to keep.

The Ryukin goldfish was developed in Japan and comes in a huge variety of colors. It is very graceful in motion, its V-shaped tail and paired anal fins giving it a real elegance.

Veiltail

The tail fin hangs in folds, the anal fin is long and delicate, and the dorsal fin is very tall in veiltails. They are slow swimmers and can easily become damaged on sharp objects, but they are graceful and beautiful.

Originally bred in the United States, veiltail goldfish should have a short and rounded body with a smooth outline. The trailing edge of the caudal fin to be free from forking or pointed lobes. The caudal fin should be divided, flowing, and at least three-quarters of the body length.

Moor

This goldfish, sometimes called the black moor, is jet black and has the outline of a veiltail. The moor goldfish is one of the more rounded or egg-shaped fancy gold fish.

The rounded body shape of this beautiful fish is enhanced by large bulbous eyes protruding from the sides of its head, metallic scales that give it a deep velvety black color, and long, flowing fins.

Lionhead

The lionhead goldfish is by far the most popular and well known of the goldfish that lack a dorsal fin.

Rather than having the long, slender body of the common goldfish or the shubunkins, the lionhead is one of the more rounded or egg-shaped fancy goldfish. It has a double caudal fin and a double anal fin. It is named because of the raspberry-like growth on its head that looks a little like a lion's mane. The lionhead is attractive, but a poor swimmer.

49

Fantail

One of the few fancy varieties to thrive in a pond, as it tolerates low temperatures well. It is similar in appearance to the ryukin, but with a shorter fan-shaped tail and a rounder body.

Fantails are a good fancy variety for beginners. They come in several colors and scale types.

Oranda

The oranda was created by crossbreeding the veiltail with the lionhead. It has an egg-shaped body with a flowing pair of caudal fins.

Like the lionhead, the oranda also has a growth or **wen** on its head that is raspberry like in appearance. Similar in shape to the lionhead, it does have a dorsal fin. It comes in a variety of colors including calico, orange, red, blue, chocolate, bronze, white, silver, red-white, red-black, panda-colored, and tricolor. It can grow to a length of 8 to 12 inches (20-30 cm).

53

Bubble Eye

The bubble eye is a small variety of fancy goldfish with upward-pointing eyes with two large fluid-filled sacs alongside them.

The bubbles are fragile and the fish should be kept separate from boisterous types, and away from sharp tank decor. This fish lacks a dorsal fin and consequently is a poor swimmer. In general, the bubble eye is a delicate variety, and should not be kept with other fish.

Pompom

Named for the two "cheerleader" pompoms that are positioned above each nostril, this goldfish comes in a variety of colors. The pompom's body shape and fins are similar to the lionhead, but instead of a head growth it has nasal outgrowths.

The extent of the nasal outgrowths, which are enlargements of the nasal septum, vary in pompon goldfish. In some, the outgrowths hang down past the mouth.

If you plan to keep more than one fancy variety, the best combination is veiltails, ryukins, and orandas. Moors and bubble eyes can also be kept together.

In the Wild

The closest wild relatives of the goldfish are the crucian and the gibel, species of carp, commonly found in lakes and rivers in many parts of Europe and Asia.

During the winter months they go into semi-hibernation, sinking to the bottom and encasing themselves in mud. Goldfish seem to have inherited this ability to survive during cold periods.

Wild crucians and gibels **spawn** in the spring and early summer, with an individual female laying as many as 250,000 eggs.

The gibel may reach around 12 inches (30 cm) in lengths but crucians can grow to almost double that length and weigh as much as 7 pounds (3 kg).

The Aquarium

If you are a first-time fish keeper, you will probably keep your goldfish indoors in an aquarium.

Goldfish must have enough room to swim so they do not feel overcrowded. There must also be enough oxygen in the water for the fish to remain healthy. The best plan is to buy the biggest tank you can afford, and then don't overcrowd it with fish.

Home sweet home—
your goldfish's
aquarium.

Positioning the Tank

When a tank is full of water it will be very heavy, so you must have a sturdy table or shelf to put it on. The tank will also need to be near an electrical outlet. When you are deciding where to put your aquarium, consider the following:

- The main living room is a great place for your aquarium, as you will have the most chance to enjoy it. Just make sure your goldfish do not get too much attention from family members or from visitors who may tap on the glass and upset the fish.

- The kitchen is not ideal, as cooking and cleaning fumes could be harmful to your fish.

- The bathroom must be ruled out, as the temperature changes too much.

- Do not position your aquarium close to a radiator or the temperature of the water will be affected.

- The aquarium should not be in direct sunlight, or it will be overrun with **algae**, a green plant that grows on the sides of the tank.

The small aquariums here are suitable for just one or two small goldfish.

How Many?

In the wild, small fish swim in schools, since this makes it harder for a predator to attack them. A single goldfish may be safe in your aquarium, but it will not be happy because it will feel as though it is always in danger. You should always keep more than one goldfish, but be careful not to get too many.

Goldfish hate to be overcrowded, and the water will get very dirty if there are too many fish. As a general rule, you can keep one inch (2.5 cm) of fish per liter of water. More than that will result in overcrowding. The best plan is to seek advice when you buy your tank, so you can work out the right number of fish to keep.

Filters and Other Equipment

Like all living creatures, goldfish need to get rid of their waste, and unless you get a filter, the fish will be swimming around in their own toilet. A filter breaks down the waste that builds up in the water, so the fish can live in a clean, healthy tank.

There are different types of filters, which can either be attached to the side of the tank, under the tank as an external filter or lie, or underneath the gravel surface. All filters are powered by electricity either directly or indirectly, and need to be fitted carefully.

Bright lights

You do not need lighting in your aquarium, but it does look good, particularly in the evening. Many tanks come with a hood that is fitted with a fluorescent light tube, and you can switch on the lighting for 10-12 hours a day. Do not use very bright lights, or leave them on too long, or you will have problems with algae.

Pet safe

If you have another pet, make sure you buy a cover or hood for your aquarium, or your cat or dog may try its paw at fishing. Even if the pet does not succeed, a paw dipped in the water would be very frightening for your goldfish.

Be careful

The filter and lighting are both powered by electricity, so take care when you put the equipment. A responsible adult should always take charge to switch the lighting on or off, and keep track of when the filter needs to be cleaned. Clean the filter **medium** with water removed from the aquarium, because it is colonized with helpful bacteria that keep the filter working properly.

Keep It Clean

If you do not have a filter, you will need to take extra steps to keep aquarium water clean.

- Remove a cup or two of water every couple of days and replace with water that is at room temperature and has been treated with a dechlorinator.

- Make a partial water change every week of around 20 percent using dechlorinated water that has been allowed to reach room temperature.

- Clean all ornaments in the tank once a week, but do not use detergent, just wash them under running tap water.

Keep it clean—
aquarium care

Tank Set-up

Tank Set-up

Once you have your electrical equipment fitted, you can create an environment that looks good and is safe for your goldfish.

Substrate material

The bottom of the tank should be covered with gravel. This can be brightly colored, or natural looking. Wash the gravel in water (no detergent!) before you put it into the tank, and then make a slope going from the back of the tank to the front. If you are using an under-gravel filter, cover it with 3 to 4 inches (7 to 10 cm) of gravel.

Decoration

You can really go to town when it comes to choosing ornaments for your tank. You may like fairytale castles and deep-sea divers, or you may prefer rocks and natural wood. Goldfish seem to like rocks with caves, which they can swim through.

Before buying your tank decorations, check that the items are suitable for a goldfish aquarium. This is important if you are planning to keep fancy goldfish, as their fins can get damaged on the sharp edges of rocks or ornaments.

Don't collect items from nature, pretty as they may seem. They can give off chemicals that kill your goldfish. Stick to items you buy at the aquarium store.

Plants

Goldfish are great nibblers. Some fish keepers choose artificial plants for the tank, which will not need replacing. But your aquarium will benefit from having living plants—and the goldfish will enjoy hiding among the plants as well as having an occasional snack!

A number of plants thrive in coldwater tanks. They include the following:

- Vallis (Vallisneria spiralis): An excellent plant for beginners, but will get eaten by your fish. Needs good lighting to thrive.

- Egeria densa: A member of the waterweed family, this is an excellent plant for beginners. Needs good lighting and will get eaten by your fish.

- Java fern (Microsorium): A broad-leafed plant that grows from a thick root. Not edible and may suffer at temperatures lower than 59° F (15° C).

Plant your tank when
it is half-full of water
so that you will be able
to position your plants
without getting soaked!

Filling Up

You can't just turn on the tap and fill up your tank with water. A healthy aquarium needs high-quality water. Tap water is okay for us to use, but it is not suitable for fish living in an aquarium.

- It may contain a number of different chemicals, such as chlorine and chloramine, which are harmful to fish.

- There may be high levels of nitrates and phosphates in the water, which encourage algae growth.

These problems can be solved by using a chemical dechlorinator, which prepares tap water for use in an aquarium. It is available from most pet and aquarium and pet supply stores.

Before adding water to the tank, you will need to calculate how much dechlorinator you need to add to the water, based on how much water it holds. When you fill the tank, make a note of the volume of water you add.

When you fill your tank, place a small saucer on the gravel surface, then gently pour the water on to it. This will help the water to spread evenly, so the gravel is not disturbed and the ornaments do not fall over.

Temperature

Do not use hot water from the tap when you are filling your tank. Instead, pour in cold

water. This will rise to room temperature gradually, which will suit most varieties of goldfish.

Be patient

Hang on before you rush off to buy your goldfish! Once you have set up your aquarium, wait at least a week before you introduce the fish. This gives time for the water to come to room temperature, and allows the water to reach the right chemical balance. This can be checked by using a simple test kit, which is available from all good aquarium stores. Follow the printed in-structions and test the water for **pH**, ammonia, nitrate, and nitrite levels to see if it is suitable for the fish. There are products available from your pet store that will add "good" bacteria to your tank when you're set-ting it up. They will accelerate the nitrogen cycle (more about that on the next page) of the filter and water. As with all additives to your aquarium, ensure that you read the directions and calculate the water volume of your tank so that you add the correct amount.

Understand the Nitrogen Cycle

Every newly set up aquarium goes through a process of establishing beneficial bacterial colonies. Older aquariums also go through periods during which the bacterial colonies fluctuate. Failure to understand this process is the largest contributing factor to the loss of fish. Learning what the nitrogen cycle is, and how to deal with critical periods during tit, will greatly increase your chances of successful fishkeeping.

The waste problem

Unlike nature, an aquarium is a closed environment. All the wastes excreted from the fish, uneaten food, and decaying plants stay inside the tank. If nothing eliminated those wastes, your beautiful aquarium would turn into a sewer in no time at all.

Actually, for a short period of time, a new aquarium does become toxic. The water may look clear, but don't be fooled. It's loaded with toxins. Sounds awful, doesn't it? Fortunately, bacteria that are capable of converting wastes to safer by-products begin growing in the tank as soon as fish are added. Unfortunately, there aren't enough bacteria to eliminate all the toxins immediately (as mentioned earlier, there are products available that can assist and accelerate the process), so for a period of several weeks your fish are at risk.

However, they need not suffer. Armed with an understanding of how the nitrogen cycle works and knowing the proper steps to take, you can sail through the break-in cycle with very few problems.

When you are starting a new tank, buy a single goldfish and allow it to settle in for a week or two, before introducing more fish. It is best to wait until the nitrogen cycle is complete before adding more fish.

Stages of the nitrogen cycle

There are three stages of the nitrogen cycle, they present different challenges.

Initial stage

The cycle begins the fish is introduced to the aquarium. It's feces, urine, as well as any uneaten food, are quickly broken down into either ionized or unionized ammonia. The ionized form, ammonium ($NH4$), is present if the pH is below 7, and is not toxic to fish. The unionized form, ammonia ($NH3$), is present if the pH is 7 or above, and is highly toxic to fish. Any amount of unionized ammonia ($NH3$) is dangerous, however, once the levels reach 2 parts per million (ppm), the fish are in grave danger. Ammonia levels usually begin rising by the third day after fish have been introduced.

Second stage

During this stage, Nitrosomonas bacteria oxidize the ammonia, eliminating it. However, the by-product of ammonia oxidation is nitrite, which is also highly toxic to fish.

Nitrite levels usually begin rising by the end of the first week after fish have been introduced.

Third stage

In the last stage of the cycle, Nitrobacter bacteria convert the nitrites into nitrates. Nitrates are not highly toxic to fish in low to moderate levels. Routine partial water changes will keep the nitrate levels within the safe range. Established tanks should be tested for nitrates every few months to ensure that levels are not becoming extremely high. Of course, nitrates are also great for plant growth, so a planted aquarium will thrive when the nitrogen cycle has reached this point.

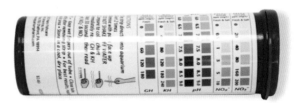

Now that you know what is happening, what should you do? Simple steps such as testing and changing the water will help you manage the nitrogen cycle without losing your fish.

The key to success is testing the water for ammonia and nitrites, and taking action quickly when problems occur. You can buy a testing kit from your local aquarium store.

Test for ammonia

Begin testing on day three after adding the fish, and continue every day until the ammonia begins to drop. After it begins to fall, continue testing every other day until the ammonia reaches zero. If at any time your fish show signs of distress, such as rapid breathing (gilling), clamped fins, erratic swimming, or hanging at the surface for air, take immediate action to lower the ammonia level. Perform an immediate 25 to 50 percent water change and test daily until levels drop.

Test for nitrites

Begin testing one week after adding the fish. Continue testing every second or third day, until it reaches zero. Again, if your fish appeared distressed, test for nitrite. If levels are elevated, perform an immediate 25-50 percent water change and test daily until levels drop.

What Not to Do!

- Don't add more fish—wait until the cycle is completed.

- Don't change the filter media—the beneficial bacteria are growing there. Don't disturb them until they have become well established. As mentioned earlier, use water removed from the tank when doing a water change to clean your filter media.

- Don't overfeed the fish—when in doubt, underfeed your fish. Remember that anything going into the tank will produce waste one way or another.

- Don't try to alter the pH—the beneficial bacteria can be affected by changes in pH. Unless there is a serious problem with the pH, leave it alone during the startup cycle process

What not to do!
Goldfish care tips.

Looking Good!

When you're buying goldfish, look at them carefully for these signs of good health:

Eyes

The eyes should be bright and clear.

Dorsal fin

This should be straight, and standing upright as the fish swims.

Body

The body should be well-rounded.

Mouth

The fish should open its mouth, but should not appear to be gulping for air.

Gills

All the gills should be red-colored, and showing steady movement.

Pelvic fins

These should extend out to the sides.

Vent

There should be no sign of sticky waste, or soreness.

Movement

The fish should swim easily. A fish that wobbles or tilts, or rests on the bottom, could be sick.

Scales

The scales should be free from spots or bumps, or woolly-looking patches of fungus.

Color

The color of the fish should be dense and even.

At last it is time to go and buy your goldfish. There are many varieties to choose from, so take your time and observe the fish. If you are planning to keep more than one variety, ask for advice so you get the right mix. Remember, fancy goldfish are not as hardy as the single-tailed varieties.

Arriving Home

Goldfish

The goldfish you choose will be put in a plastic bag full of water for the journey home. Do not pour your fish straight into the tank the minute you arrive home. Goldfish hate shocks, such as a sudden change in temperature. You need to wait until the water in the bag is the same temperature as the tank water.

- Open the top of the bag and leave it floating in the tank.

- After 20 minutes, mix the water in the tank with the water in the bag, to minimize pH shock, leave the fish in the bag five minutes more. Then gently then release the fish into your tank.

Feeding Fish

Fish that live in the wild must find their own food, but aquarium fish rely on you to provide the correct diet. Feed your goldfish twice a day, and give only as much food as they will eat within 2 minutes. A floating feeding ring will keep the food in one place so your fish can find it easily.

Goldfish are hardy fish and are not too fussy about the food they eat. They need carbohydrates and vitamins to help them grow and to fight disease. They also need a small amount of protein so they can build muscle. Fortunately, we do not have to worry about preparing food that has all these nutrients in the correct balance. It comes ready-made.

Dried food

Goldfish food comes in a dried flakes, granules, or pellets. There are many different brands available, but it is important that you read the label and make sure you are buying food that is especially for goldfish.

Supplements

Wild or pond-living goldfish will eat large amounts of plants or weeds, which are not available to an aquarium fish. In order to give your goldfish this type of food (and to save your aquarium plants), you can provide a slice of cucumber, or hang some freshly washed lettuce inside the tank. Your goldfish will love it.

Frozen food

Pond-living goldfish eat shrimps, aquatic worms, and snails, and aquarium fish will certainly enjoy live food, such as bloodworm, daphnia, or brine shrimp. But these live foods may bring germs with them, introducing disease to your aquarium. Frozen food provides your goldfish with the benefits of live food, without as much risk of introducing disease.

Overfeeding

Don't overfeed your goldfish. They will always be keen to come to the surface when you offer food, but too much food is very bad for them. Goldfish will develop health problems if they eat too much, and leftover food will pollute the water, which could kill the fish.

Vacation

You can buy slow-releasing food, which will
last your goldfish for a short period, but ideally
someone should keep an eye on your fish while
you are away. Problems can arise when a friend
looks after your fish if they overfeed. Make sure
that the person looking after your fish knows how
much to feed and when!

Goldfish Care

If you keep a close check on your aquarium, you can spot any signs of trouble at an early stage.

When you feed your goldfish, take a few minutes to study your fish to see if they all appear healthy. Check that the filter is operating, and have a quick look to see if any plants have been uprooted.

Quick guide to goldfish care

Testing the water

The water needs to be tested every week to make sure it is suitable for your goldfish. Use a test kit that will indicate if there is too much ammonia, nitrite, or nitrate in the water.

Water changes

If the water test shows an incorrect balance, you will need to make a water change. Generally, fishkeepers change some of the water every two weeks so that the tank is clean and healthy. If you change the water regularly, you will only need to remove 10 to 20 percent of the water at a time, which is much easier than making a complete change.

The easiest way to change water is to buy a gravel cleaner, which is specially made so that it vacuums the gravel, and sucks water out of the tank at the same time.

Before you start siphoning off the dirty water, you need to prepare a bucket of clean water. This will need to stand for a couple of hours so that it reaches room temperature. You will also need to add the appropriate amount of dechlorinator.

Filter maintenance

Keeping your filter in good working order is one of the most important tasks you can do to keep your aquarium water clean. Follow the manufacturer's guidelines for effective maintenance.

Algae growth

Algae grows on the sides of the tank, particularly if the tank is in direct sunlight, or if you leave the lighting on for long periods. Algae is not harmful to goldfish, but it does spoil the look of the aquarium. It can be removed quite easily by using an algae scraper once a week.

Fish Behavior

**Watch out for the signs that tell you how
your goldfish are feeling.**

Happy goldfish

A contented goldfish will be active in the tank, swimming easily between the plants and rocks, and coming
to the surface to feed. Its fins will be free flowing, and
it will appear bright and alert.

Pictured below:
bubble eye goldfish &
calico Oranda goldfish.

Stressed goldfish

Fish are very sensitive, and they will show signs of stress if their environment is not to their liking. It has been calculated that 90 percent of problems are due to water quality, so make sure that you test the water regularly.

Other reasons why a goldfish may be feeling stressed include overcrowding, or too few plants in the tank so that there are not enough places for the goldfish to hide.

A stressed fish will:

- Swim with its fins held tight to the body.

- Hang in corners, head down or up.

- Look nervous, as though it is trying to escape.

- Show no interest in food.

- Appear lighter or darker in color than usual.

Sleeping goldfish

As goldfish have no eyelids, they cannot close their eyes when they sleep. A sleeping goldfish will sink to a low position in the water, usually somewhere out of sight, and will turn a paler color.

Greetings

When you approach the tank, you may see your goldfish rise to the surface. This is the fish's way of saying hello!

You may see your goldfish tip up, with its head resting on the bottom of the tank and its tail held high. The goldfish has found some food, and its tail is a signal so other goldfish will swim over and enjoy the feast.

Health
Problems

Goldfish are hardier than most types of fish, and many health problems are curable if you can get the diagnosis right.

B y far the biggest cause of health problems in gold-fish is poor water quality—pollution as a result of overfeeding, too many fish, poor tap water, or faulty equipment—so your first step should always be to test the water.

Test for ammonia and nitrites first, then pH and nitrates. One of the keys to keeping your fish healthy is to check them regularly. The more often you observe them, the more likely you are to spot unusual behavior or other symptoms.

Signs of Poor Health

- Marks on the mouth or lips.

- Eyes that are dull or cloudy.

- Black, red or white marks (other than normal coloring) on the body or fins.

- Scales slightly raised from the body.

- Swimming on the spot.

- Fins held down and close to the body.

- Gasping at the surface.

Skin Complaints

Fin/tail rot and mouth fungus

These are the result of bacterial infection, usually caused by poor water quality. White marks on the edges of the fins and mouth are followed by a reddening of the area and, eventually, rotting away. Work on fixing the water quality.

Sores and ulcers

These may be caused by bacteria or a viral infection, sometimes on the site of an old wound. They can often be cured by adding an off-the-shelf remedy from the aquarium store to the water, though if a virus is involved the condition may recur as the fish's immune system is weakened. In extreme cases, your veterinarian will prescribe an antibiotic to add to the water.

Cuts and scrapes

These most commonly occur when fish are chasing, or being chased, at high speed. For this reason you need to be careful that any decor you add to your tank does not have sharp edges.

Dead skin and scales resulting from a scrape will turn white; if you spot this, treat the water with an off-the-shelf remedy. As above, extreme cases may need an antibiotic from your veterinarian.

Fungal infections

These often develop on a wound, feeding on the damaged skin or scales. They will appear as white growths on the skin, often looking like strands or clumps of cotton. They are relatively easy to cure. Ask about remedies at your aquarium store.

Parasitic Infections

Whitespot

Whitespot is a **parasite** that burrows under a gold-fish's skin, forming white pin-headed cysts. It can also cause gill irritation, which may leave your fish gasping at the surface.

It is simple to cure with a chemical treatment, but it is necessary to treat the whole of the aquarium or pond rather than individual fish.

Fish lice

The fish louse attaches itself to your goldfish's body and sucks juices from it. Flat and scale-like in apear-ance, the fish louse is a large parasite and it is quite easy to spot. They don't respond well to antiparasitic treatments and are best removed individually if pos-sible. They can be hard to control in ponds because the egg stage is resistant to most chemicals.

Leeches

These are more of a problem in ponds than in the aquarium. They are thin worm-like creatures, that fix themselves to the skin and suck nourishment from the fish.

They are almost impossible to eradicate completely from a pond, though a chemical treatment from your aquarium or pond supply store will keep them under control.

Find Out More

Books

Boruchowitz, David E. *The Simple Guide to Freshwater Aquariums*. TFH Publications, 2001.

Russell-Davies, Julia. *Mini Encyclopedia of Goldfish*. Firefly Books, 2015.

Skomal, Gregory. *Goldfish: Your Happy Healthy Pet*. Howell Book House, 2007.

Web Sites

www.americangoldfish1.org
American Goldfish Association is a club dedicated to caring for, breeding, and showing goldfish. It contains information about all the varieties, and where you can find goldfish shows.

goldfishkeepers.com
Goldfish Keepers connects hobbyists, breeders, and sellers, who offer tips and advice from the most basic to the most advanced.

 # Words to Understand

algae   a simple, single-celled plant

gill   the breathing organ of fishes that takes oxygen from the water

hardy   strong; able to live in difficult conditions

lateral   along the sides

medium   in aquarium filters, the substance on which the helpful bacteria grows

parasite   an organism that takes what it needs from the host it lives on

pH   a measure of how acid or alkaline something is

school   a large group of animals that stay together in the water

spawn   releasing eggs to reproduce

toxic   poisonous; deadly to living things

wen   a natural swelling or growth on the top of the goldfish's head

Index